WASHINGTON'S
FAREWELL
ADDRESS

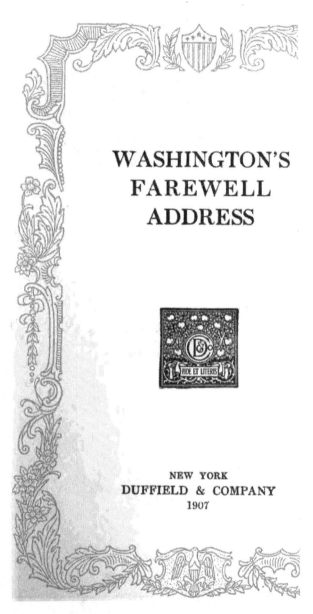

NEW YORK
DUFFIELD & COMPANY
1907

Copyright, 1907, by

DUFFIELD & COMPANY

Published August, 1907

WASHINGTON'S FAREWELL ADDRESS

Friends, and Fellow-Citizens:

The period for the new election of a Citizen, to administer the Executive Government of the United States, being not far distant, and the time actually arrived, when your thoughts must be employed in designating the person, who is to be clothed with that important trust, it appears to me proper, especially as it may conduce to a more distinct expression of the public voice, that I should now apprise you of the resolution I have formed to decline being considered among the number of those, out of whom a choice is to be made.

I beg you, at the same time, to do me the justice to be assured, that this resolution has not been taken, without a strict regard to all the considerations appertaining to the relation, which binds a dutiful citizen to his country—and that, in withdrawing the tender of service which silence in my situation might imply, I am influenced by no diminution of zeal for your future interest, no deficiency of grateful respect for your past kindness; but am supported by a full conviction that the step is compatible with both.

The acceptance of, and continuance hitherto in, the office to which your suffrages have twice called me, have been a uniform sacrifice of inclination to the opinion of duty, and to a deference for what appeared to be your desire. I constantly hoped, that it would have been much earlier in my power, consistently with motives, which I was not at liberty to disregard, to return to that retirement, from which I had been reluctantly drawn. The strength of my inclination to do this, previous to the last election, had even led to the preparation of an address to declare it to you; but mature reflection on the then perplexed and critical posture of our affairs with foreign Nations, and the unanimous advice of persons entitled to my confidence, impelled me to abandon the idea.

I rejoice that the state of your concerns, external as well as internal, no longer renders the pursuit of inclination incompatible with the sentiment of duty or propriety; and am persuaded, whatever partiality may be retained for my services, that in the present circumstances of our country you will not disapprove my determination to retire.

The impressions, with which I first undertook the arduous trust, were explained on the proper occasion. In the discharge of this trust, I will only say, that I have, with good intentions, contributed towards the organization and administration of the government, the best exertions of which a very fallible judgment was capable. Not unconscious, in the outset, of the inferiority of my qualifications, experience in my own eyes, perhaps still more in the eyes of others, has strengthened the motives to diffidence of myself; and every day the increasing weight of years admonishes me more and more, that the shade of retirement is as necessary to me as it will be welcome. Satisfied, that, if any circumstances have given peculiar value to my services, they were temporary, I have the consolation to believe, that, while choice and prudence invite me to quit the political scene, patriotism does not forbid it.

In looking forward to the moment, which is intended to terminate the career of my public life, my feelings do not permit me to suspend the deep acknowledgment of that debt of gratitude, which I owe to my beloved country—for the many honors it has conferred upon me; still more for the stedfast confidence with which it has supported me; and for the opportunities I have thence enjoyed of manifesting my inviolable attachment, by

6

services faithful and persevering, though in usefulness unequal to my zeal. If benefits have resulted to our country from these services, let it always be remembered to your praise, and as an instructive example in our annals, that under circumstances in which the Passions agitated in every direction were liable to mislead, amidst appearances somewhat dubious, vicissitudes of fortune often discouraging —in situations in which not unfrequently want of success has countenanced the spirit of criticism, the constancy of your support was the essential prop of the efforts and a guarantee of the plans by which

they were effected. Profound-
ly penetrated with this idea, I
shall carry it with me to the
grave, as a strong incitement
to unceasing vows that
Heaven may continue to you
the choicest tokens of its
beneficence—that your union
and brotherly affection may be
perpetual—that the free constitution, which is the work of
your hands, may be sacredly
maintained—that its administration in every department
may be stamped with wisdom
and virtue—that, in fine, the
happiness of the people of
these States, under the au-
spices of liberty, may be made
complete, by so careful a
preservation and so prudent a

use of this blessing as will acquire to them the glory of recommending it to the applause, the affection, and adoption of every nation, which is yet a stranger to it.

Here, perhaps, I ought to stop. But a solicitude for your welfare, which cannot end but with my life, and the apprehension of danger, natural to that solicitude, urge me on an occasion like the present, to offer to your solemn contemplation, and to recommend to your frequent review, some sentiments, which are the result of much reflection, of no inconsiderable observation, and which appear to me all important to the permanency of your felicity as a People. These will be offered to you with the more freedom, as you can only see in them the disinterested warnings of a parting friend, who can possibly have no personal motive to bias his counsels. Nor can I forget, as an encouragement to it, your indulgent reception of my sentiments on a former and not dissimilar occasion.

Interwoven as is the love of liberty with every ligament of your hearts, no recommendation of mine is necessary to fortify or confirm the attachment.

The Unity of Government which constitutes you one people, is also now dear to you.

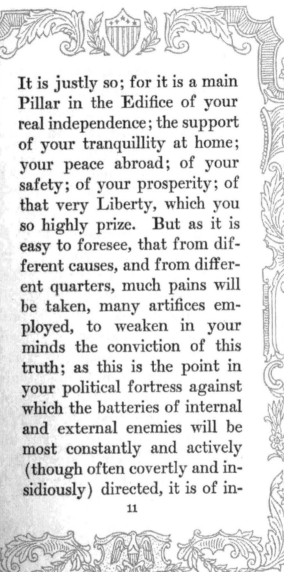

It is justly so; for it is a main Pillar in the Edifice of your real independence; the support of your tranquillity at home; your peace abroad; of your safety; of your prosperity; of that very Liberty, which you so highly prize. But as it is easy to foresee, that from different causes, and from different quarters, much pains will be taken, many artifices employed, to weaken in your minds the conviction of this truth; as this is the point in your political fortress against which the batteries of internal and external enemies will be most constantly and actively (though often covertly and insidiously) directed, it is of in-

11

finite moment, that you should
properly estimate the immense
value of your national Union
to your collective and individual happiness; that you should
cherish a cordial, habitual, and
immoveable attachment to it;
accustoming yourselves to
think and speak of it as of the
Palladium of your political
safety and prosperity; watch-
ing for its preservation with
jealous anxiety; discounte-
nancing whatever may sug-
gest even a suspicion that it
can in any event be abandoned,
and indignantly frowning
upon the first dawning of
every attempt to alienate any
portion of our Country from
the rest, or to enfeeble the

sacred ties which now link together the various parts.

For this you have every inducement of sympathy and interest. Citizens by birth or choice of a common country, that country has a right to concentrate your affections. The name of AMERICAN, which belongs to you, in your national capacity, must always exalt the just pride of Patriotism, more than any appellation derived from local discriminations. With slight shades of difference, you have the same Religion, Manners, Habits, and political Principles. You have in a common cause fought and triumphed together. The Independence and Liberty you possess are the work of joint councils, and joint efforts—of common dangers, sufferings and successes.

But these considerations, however powerfully they address themselves to your sensibility, are greatly outweighed by those which apply more immediately to your Interest. Here every portion of our country finds the most commanding motives for carefully guarding and preserving the Union of the whole.

The *North* in an unrestrained intercourse with the *South,* protected by the equal Laws of a common government, finds in the productions of the latter great additional

14

resources of maritime and commercial enterprise—and precious materials of manufacturing industry. The *South* in the same intercourse, benefiting by the agency of the *North,* sees its agriculture grow and its commerce expand. Turning partly into its own channels the seamen of the *North,* it finds its particular navigation envigorated; and, while it contributes, in different ways, to nourish and increase the general mass of the national navigation, it looks forward to the protection of a maritime strength to which itself is unequally adapted. The *East,* in a like intercourse with the *West,* already finds, and in the progressive improvement of interior communications, by land and water, will more and more find, a valuable vent for the commodities which it brings from abroad, or manufactures at home. The *West* derives from the *East* supplies requisite to its growth and comfort, and what is perhaps of still greater consequence, it must of necessity owe the *secure* enjoyment of indispensable *outlets* for its own productions to the weight, influence, and the future maritime strength of the Atlantic side of the Union, directed by an indissoluble community of interests, as *one Nation*. Any other tenure by which the

West can hold this essential advantage, whether derived from its own separate strength or from an apostate and unnatural connexion with any foreign Power, must be intrinsically precarious.

While then every part of our Country thus feels an immediate and particular interest in Union, all the parts combined cannot fail to find in the united mass of means and efforts greater strength, greater resource, proportionably greater security from external danger, a less frequent interruption of their Peace by foreign Nations; and, what is of inestimable value! they must derive from Union an exemp-

17

tion from those broils and wars between themselves, which so frequently afflict neighbouring countries, not tied together by the same government; which their own rivalships alone would be sufficient to produce; but which opposite foreign alliances, attachments and intrigues would stimulate and embitter. Hence likewise they will avoid the necessity of those overgrown Military establishments, which under any form of government, are inauspicious to liberty, and which are to be regarded as particularly hostile to Republican Liberty: In this sense it is, that, your Union ought to be considered as a main prop of your liberty, and that the love of the one ought to endear to you the preservation of the other.

These considerations speak a persuasive language to every reflecting and virtuous mind, and exhibit the continuance of the UNION as a primary object of Patriotic desire. Is there a doubt, whether a common government can embrace so large a sphere? Let experience solve it. To listen to mere speculation in such a case were criminal. We are authorized to hope that a proper organization of the whole, with the auxiliary agency of governments for the respective subdivisions, will afford a happy issue to the experiment. 'Tis well worth a fair and full experiment. With such powerful and obvious motives to Union, affecting all parts of our country, while experience shall not have demonstrated its impracticability, there will always be reason to distrust the patriotism of those, who in any quarter may endeavor to weaken its bands.

In contemplating the causes which may disturb our Union, it occurs as matter of serious concern, that any ground should have been furnished for characterizing parties by *Geographical* discriminations — *Northern* and *Southern—Atlantic* and *Western,* whence designing men may endeavor to excite a belief, that there is a real difference of local interests and views.

One of the expedients of Party to acquire influence, within particular districts, is to misrepresent the opinions and aims of other districts. You cannot shield yourselves too much against the jealousies and heart burnings which spring from these misrepresentations. They tend to render alien to each other those who ought to be bound together by fraternal affection. The inhabitants of our Western country have lately had a useful lesson on this head. They have seen, in the negotiation by the Executive, and in the

unanimous ratification by
the Senate, of the Treaty
with Spain, and in the uni-
versal satisfaction at that
event, throughout the United
States, a decisive proof how
unfounded were the suspicions
propagated among them of a
policy in the General Government and in the Atlantic
States unfriendly to their interests in regard to the MIS-
SISSIPPI. They have been wit-
nesses to the formation of two
Treaties, that with G. Britain,
and that with Spain, which secure to them every thing they
could desire, in respect to our
Foreign Relations, towards
confirming their prosperity.
Will it not be their wisdom to

rely for the preservation
of these advantages on the
UNION by which they were
procured? Will they not
henceforth be deaf to those ad-
visers, if such there are, who
would sever them from their
Brethren, and connect them
with Aliens?

To the efficacy and permanency of your Union, a Government for the whole is indispensable. No alliances however strict between the parts
can be an adequate substitute.
They must inevitably experience the infractions and inter-
ruptions which all alliances in
all times have experienced.
Sensible of this momentous
truth, you have improved upon

23

your first essay, by the adoption of a Constitution of Government, better calculated than your former for an intimate Union, and for the efficacious management of your common concerns. This government, the offspring of our own choice uninfluenced and unawed, adopted upon full investigation and mature deliberation, completely free in its principles, in the distribution of its powers, uniting security with energy, and containing within itself a provision for its own amendment, has a just claim to your confidence and your support. Respect for its authority, compliance with its Laws, acquiescence in its measures, are duties enjoined by the fundamental maxims of true Liberty. The basis of our political systems is the right of the people to make and to alter their Constitutions of Government. But the constitution which at any time exists, 'till changed by an explicit and authentic act of the whole People, is sacredly obligatory upon all. The very idea of the power and the right of the People to establish Government, presupposes the duty of every individual to obey the established Government.

All obstructions to the execution of the Laws, all combinations and associations, under whatever plausible char-

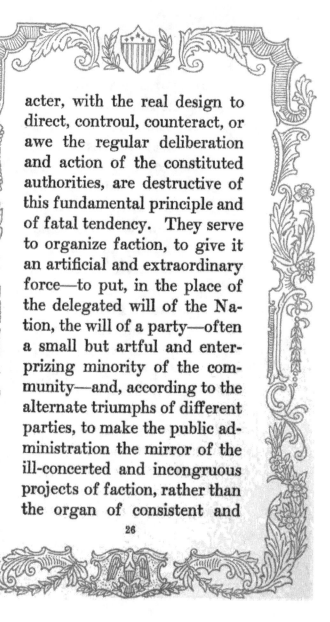

acter, with the real design to
direct, controul, counteract, or
awe the regular deliberation
and action of the constituted
authorities, are destructive of
this fundamental principle and
of fatal tendency. They serve
to organize faction, to give it
an artificial and extraordinary
force—to put, in the place of
the delegated will of the Nation, the will of a party—often
a small but artful and enter-
prizing minority of the community—and, according to the
alternate triumphs of different
parties, to make the public administration the mirror of the
ill-concerted and incongruous
projects of faction, rather than
the organ of consistent and

26

wholesome plans digested by
common councils and modified
by mutual interests. However
combinations or associations of
the above description may now
and then answer popular ends,
they are likely, in the course
of time and things, to become
potent engines, by which cun-
ning, ambitious, and unprin-
cipled men will be enabled to
subvert the Power of the People and to usurp for themselves the reins of Government; destroying afterwards
the very engines which have
lifted them to unjust do-
minion.

Towards the preservation of
your Government and the permanency of your present hap-

py state, it is requisite, not
only that you steadily discoun-
tenance irregular oppositions
to its acknowledged authority,
but also that you resist with
care the spirit of innovation
upon its principles, however
specious the pretexts. One
method of assault may be to
effect, in the forms of the Constitution, alterations which will
impair the energy of the sys-
tem, and thus to undermine
what cannot be directly over-
thrown. In all the changes to
which you may be invited, re-
member that time and habit
are at least as necessary to fix
the true character of Governments, as of other human institutions—that experience is

the surest standard, by which
to test the real tendency of
the existing Constitution of
a Country—that facility in
changes upon the credit of
mere hypothesis and opinion
exposes to perpetual change,
from the endless variety of hypothesis and opinion—and re-
member, especially, that for
the efficient management of
your common interests, in a
country so extensive as ours, a
Government of as much vigor
as is consistent with the perfect
security of Liberty is indispensable.   Liberty itself will
find in such a Government,
with powers properly dis-
tributed and adjusted, its
surest Guardian.   It is indeed

little else than a name, where
the Government is too feeble
to withstand the enterprises of
faction, to confine each member of the Society within the
limits prescribed by the laws,
and to maintain all in the secure and tranquil enjoyment
of the rights of person and
property.

I have already intimated to
you the danger of Parties in
the State, with particular
reference to the founding of
them on Geographical discriminations. Let me now take a
more comprehensive view, and
warn you in the most solemn
manner against the baneful ef-
fects of the Spirit of Party,
generally.

This Spirit, unfortunately, is inseparable from our nature, having its root in the strongest passions of the human mind. It exists under different shapes in all Governments, more or less stifled, controuled, or repressed; but, in those of the popular form, it is seen in its greatest rankness, and is truly their worst enemy.

The alternate domination of one faction over another, sharpened by the spirit of revenge natural to party dissension, which in different ages and countries has perpetrated the most horrid enormities, is itself a frightful despotism. But this leads at length to a more formal and permanent despotism. The disorders and miseries, which result, gradually incline the minds of men to seek security and repose in the absolute power of an Individual: and sooner or later the chief of some prevailing faction, more able or more fortunate than his competitors, turns this disposition to the purposes of his own elevation, on the ruins of Public Liberty.

Without looking forward to an extremity of this kind, (which nevertheless ought not to be entirely out of sight), the common and continual mischiefs of the spirit of Party are sufficient to make it the interest and duty of a wise Peo-

ple to discourage and restrain
it.

It serves always to distract
the Public Councils, and enfeeble the Public administration. It agitates the community with ill founded jealousies and false alarms, kin-
dles the animosity of one part
against another, foments oc-
casionally riot and insurrec-
tion. It opens the doors to
foreign influence and corruption, which find a facilitated
access to the Government itself through the channels of
party passions. Thus the policy and the will of one country,
are subjected to the policy and
will of another.

There is an opinion that

parties in free countries are useful checks upon the Administration of the Government, and serve to keep alive the Spirit of Liberty. This within certain limits is probably true—and in Governments of a Monarchical cast, Patriotism may look with indulgence, if not with favour, upon the spirit of party. But in those of the popular character, in Governments purely elective, it is a spirit not to be encouraged. From their natural tendency, it is certain there will always be enough of that spirit for every salutary purpose, and there being constant danger of excess, the effort ought to be, by force of public opinion, to mitigate and assuage it. A fire not to be quenched; it demands a uniform vigilance to prevent its bursting into a flame, lest, instead of warming, it should consume.

It is important, likewise, that the habits of thinking in a free country should inspire caution in those entrusted with its administration, to confine themselves within their repective constitutional spheres; avoiding in the exercise of the powers of one department to encroach upon another. The spirit of encroachment tends to consolidate the powers of all the departments in one, and thus to create, whatever

the form of government, a real
despotism. A just estimate
of that love of power, and
proneness to abuse it, which
predominates in the human
heart, is sufficient to satisfy us
of the truth of this position.
The necessity of reciprocal
checks in the exercise of political power, by dividing and
distributing it into different
depositories, and constituting
each the Guardian of the Public Weal against invasions by
the others, has been evinced by
experiments ancient and mod-
ern; some of them in our country and under our own eyes.
To preserve them must be as
necessary as to institute them.
If in the opinion of the Peo-

ple, the distribution or modification of the Constitutional powers be in any particular wrong, let it be corrected by an amendment in the way which the Constitution designates. But let there be no change by usurpation; for though this, in one instance, may be the instrument of good, it is the customary weapon by which free governments are destroyed. The precedent must always greatly overbalance in permanent evil any partial or transient benefit which the use can at any time yield.

Of all the dispositions and habits, which lead to political prosperity, Religion and morality are indispensable supports. In vain would that man claim the tribute of Patriotism, who should labour to subvert these great pillars of human happiness, these firmest props of the duties of Men and Citizens. The mere Politician, equally with the pious man, ought to respect and to cherish them. A volume could not trace all their connexions withprivate and public felicity. Let it simply be asked where is the security for property, for reputation, for life, if the sense of religious obligation *desert* the oaths, which are the instruments of investigation in Courts of Justice? And let us with caution indulge the

38

supposition, that morality can be maintained without religion. Whatever may be conceded to the influence of refined education on minds of peculiar structure — reason and experience both forbid us to expect, that national morality can prevail in exclusion of religious principle.

'Tis substantially true, that virtue or morality is a necessary spring of popular government. The rule indeed extends with more or less force to every species of Free Government. Who that is a sincere friend to it, can look with indifference upon attempts to shake the foundation of the fabric?

39

Promote, then, as of primary importance, institutions for the general diffusion of knowledge. In proportion as the structure of a government gives force to public opinion, it is essential that public opinion should be enlightened.

As a very important source of strength and security, cherish public credit. One method of preserving it is to use it as sparingly as possible—avoiding occasions of expense by cultivating peace, but remembering also that timely disbursements to prepare for danger frequently prevent much greater disbursements to repel it—avoiding likewise the accumulation of debt, not

only by shunning occasions of
expense, but by vigorous exertions in time of Peace to discharge the debts which un-
avoidable wars may have oc-
casioned, not ungenerously
throwing upon prosperity the
burthen which we ourselves
ought to bear. The execution
of these maxims belongs to
your Representatives, but it is
necessary that public opinion
should co-operate. To facili-
tate to them the performance
of their duty, it is essential
that you should practically
bear in mind, that towards the
payments of debts there must
be Revenue—that to have
Revenue there must be taxes
—that no taxes can be

devised which are not more or less inconvenient and unpleasant—that the intrinsic embarrassment inseparable from the selection of the proper objects (which is always a choice of difficulties) ought to be a decisive motive for a candid construction of the conduct of the Government in making it, and for a spirit of acquiescence in the measures for obtaining Revenue which the public exigencies may at any time dictate.

Observe good faith and justice towards all Nations. Cultivate peace and harmony with all. Religion and Morality enjoin this conduct; and can it be that good policy does not equally enjoin it? It will be worthy of a free, enlightened, and, at no distant period, a great nation, to give to mankind the magnanimous and too novel example of a People always guided by an exalted justice and benevolence. Who can doubt that in the course of time and things, the fruits of such a plan would richly repay any temporary advantages, which might be lost by a steady adherence to it? Can it be, that Providence has not connected the permanent felicity of a Nation with its virtue? The experiment, at least, is recommended by every sentiment which ennobles human nature. Alas! is it rendered impossible by its vices?

In the execution of such a plan nothing is more essential than that permanent, inveterate antipathies against particular nations and passionate attachments for others should be excluded; and that in place of them just and amicable feelings towards all should be cultivated. The Nation, which indulges towards another an habitual hatred or an habitual fondness, is in some degree a slave. It is a slave to its animosity or to its affection, either of which is sufficient to lead it astray from its duty and its interest. Antipathy in one nation against another disposes each more readily to offer insult and injury, to lay hold of slight causes of umbrage, and to be haughty and intractable, when accidental or trifling occasions of dispute occur. Hence frequent collisions, obstinate, envenomed and bloody contests. The Nation prompted by ill-will and resentment sometimes impel to War the Government, contrary to the best calculations of policy. The Government sometimes participates in the national propensity, and adopts through passion what reason would reject; at other times, it makes the animosity of the Nation subservient to projects of hostility

45

instigated by pride, ambition, and other sinister and pernicious motives. The peace often, sometimes perhaps the Liberty, of Nations has been the victim.

So likewise a passionate attachment of one Nation for another produces a variety of evils. Sympathy for the favourite nation, facilitating the illusion of an imaginary common interest in cases where no real common interest exists, and infusing into one the enmities of the other, betrays the former into a participation in the quarrels and wars of the latter, without adequate inducement or justification: It leads also to concessions to the

favourite Nation of privileges
denied to others, which is apt
doubly to injure the Nation
making the concessions; by un-
necessarily parting with what
ought to have been retained,
and by exciting jealousy, ill-
will, and a disposition to re-
taliate, in the parties from
whom equal privileges are
withheld; and it gives to ambitious, corrupted or deluded
citizens (who devote themselves to the favourite Nation) facility to betray, or sacrifice the interests of their own
country, without odium, sometimes even with popularity:
gilding with the appearances
of a virtuous sense of obligation, a commendable defer-

47

ence for public opinion, or a
laudable zeal for public good,
the base or foolish compliances
of ambition, corruption or infatuation.

As avenues to foreign influence in innumerable ways,
such attachments are particularly alarming to the truly enlightened and independent
Patriot. How many opportunities do they afford to tamper with domestic factions, to
practise the arts of seduction,
to mislead public opinion, to
influence or awe the public
councils! Such an attachment
of a small or weak, towards a
great and powerful nation,
dooms the former to be the
satellite of the latter.

Against the insidious wiles
of foreign influence, I conjure
you to believe me, fellow citizens, the jealousy of a free
people ought to be *constantly*
awake, since history and experience prove that foreign influence is one of the most baneful foes of Republican Government. But that jealousy,
to be useful must be impartial;
else it becomes the instrument
of the very influence to be
avoided, instead of a defence
against it. Excessive partiality for one foreign nation
and excessive dislike of another, cause those whom they
actuate to see danger only on
one side, and serve to veil and
even second the arts of in-

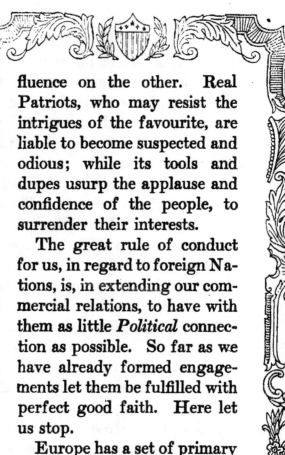

fluence on the other. Real Patriots, who may resist the intrigues of the favourite, are liable to become suspected and odious; while its tools and dupes usurp the applause and confidence of the people, to surrender their interests.

The great rule of conduct for us, in regard to foreign Nations, is, in extending our commercial relations, to have with them as little *Political* connection as possible. So far as we have already formed engagements let them be fulfilled with perfect good faith. Here let us stop.

Europe has a set of primary interests, which to us have none, or a very remote relation. Hence she must be engaged in frequent controversies, the causes of which are essentially foreign to our concerns. Hence therefore it must be unwise in us to implicate ourselves, by artificial ties, in the ordinary vicissitudes of her politics, or the ordinary combinations and collisions of her friendships, or enmities.

Our detached and distant situation invites and enables us to pursue a different course. If we remain one People, under an efficient government, the period is not far off, when we may defy material injury from external annoyance; when we may take such an attitude as will cause the neu-

trality we may at any time re-
solve upon to be scrupulously
respected. When belligerent
nations, under the impossibil-
ity of making acquisitions
upon us, will not lightly haz-
ard the giving us provocation;
when we may choose peace or
war, as our interest guided by
justice shall counsel.

Why forego the advantages
of so peculiar a situation?
Why quit our own to stand
upon foreign ground? Why,
by interweaving our destiny
with that of any part of Europe, entangle our peace and
prosperity in the toils of Eu-
ropean ambition, rivalship, interest, humour or caprice?

'Tis our true policy to steer

clear of permanent alliances, with any portion of the foreign world—so far, I mean, as we are now at liberty to do it—for let me not be understood as capable of patronizing infidelity to existing engagements. (I hold the maxim no less applicable to public than to private affairs, that honesty is the best policy). I repeat it therefore let those engagements be observed in their genuine sense. But in my opinion it is unnecessary and would be unwise to extend them.

Taking care always to keep ourselves, by suitable establishments, on a respectably defensive posture, we may safely trust to temporary alliances for extraordinary emergencies.

Harmony, liberal intercourse with all Nations, are recommended by policy, humanity and interest. But even our commercial policy should hold an equal and impartial hand: neither seeking nor granting exclusive favours or preferences; consulting the natural course of things; diffusing and diversifying by gentle means the streams of commerce, but forcing nothing; establishing with Powers so disposed—in order to give trade a stable course, to define the rights of our Merchants, and to enable the Government to support them—convention-

al rules of intercourse, the best
that present circumstances and
mutual opinion will permit;
but temporary, and liable to be
from time to time abandoned
or varied, as experience and
circumstances shall dictate;
constantly keeping in view,
that 'tis folly in one nation to
look for disinterested favours
from another—that it must
pay with a portion of its independence for whatever it
may accept under that character—that by such acceptance, it may place itself in the
condition of having given
equivalents for nominal favours and yet of being re-
proached with ingratitude for
not giving more. There can

be no greater error than to expect, or calculate upon real
favours from Nation to Nation. 'Tis an illusion which
experience must cure, which a
just pride ought to discard.

In offering to you, my
Countrymen, these counsels of
an old and affectionate friend,
I dare not hope they will make
the strong and lasting impres-
sion I could wish—that they
will controul the usual current
of the passions, or prevent our
Nation from running the
course which has hitherto
marked the destiny of Nations.
But if I may even flatter myself, that they may be produc-
tive of some partial benefit;
some occasional good; that

they may now and then recur
to moderate the fury of party
spirit, to warn against the mischiefs of foreign intrigue, to
guard against the impostures
of pretended patriotism, this
hope will be a full recompense
for the solicitude for your welfare, by which they have been
dictated.

How far in the discharge of
my official duties, I have been
guided by the principles which
have been delineated, the public Records and other evi-
dences of my conduct must
witness to You, and to the
World. To myself, the assur-
ance of my own conscience is,
that I have at least believed
myself to be guided by them.

In relation to the still sub-
sisting War in Europe, my
Proclamation of the 22d of
April, 1793, is the index to my
plan. Sanctioned by your ap-
proving voice and by that of
Your Representatives in both
Houses of Congress, the spirit
of that measure has continual-
ly governed me—uninfluenced
by any attempts to deter or
divert me from it.

After deliberate examina-
tion with the aid of the best
lights I could obtain, I was
well satisfied that our country,
under all the circumstances of
the case, had a right to take,
and was bound in duty and interest to take, a Neutral position. Having taken it, I de-

termined, as far as should depend upon me, to maintain it, with moderation, perseverance and firmness.

The considerations which respect the right to hold this conduct, it is not necessary on this occasion to detail. I will only observe, that according to my understanding of the matter, that right, so far from being denied by any of the Belligerent Powers, has been virtually admitted by all.

The duty of holding a neutral conduct may be inferred, without anything more, from the obligation which justice and humanity impose on every Nation, in cases in which it is free to act, to maintain inviolate the relations of Peace and Amity towards other Nations.

The inducements of interest for observing that conduct will best be referred to your own reflections and experience. With me, a predominant motive has been to endeavour to gain time to our country to settle and mature its yet recent institutions, and to progress without interruption to that degree of strength and consistency, which is necessary to give it, humanly speaking, the command of its own fortunes.

Though, in reviewing the incidents of my Administration, I am unconscious of intentional error—I am nevertheless too sensible of my defects not to think it probable that I may have committed many errors. Whatever they may be I fervently beseech the Almighty to avert or mitigate the evils to which they may tend. I shall also carry with me the hope that my country will never cease to view them with indulgence; and that after forty-five years of my life dedicated to its service, with an upright zeal, the faults of incompetent abilities will be consigned to oblivion, as myself must soon be to the mansions of rest.

Relying on its kindness in this as in other things, and actuated by that fervent love towards it, which is so natural to a man, who views in it the native soil of himself and his progenitors for several generations; I anticipate with pleasing expectation that retreat, in which I promise myself to realize, without alloy, the sweet enjoyment of partaking, in the midst of my fellow-citizens, the benign influence of good Laws under a free Government—the ever favourite object of my heart, and the happy reward, as I trust, of our mutual cares, labours and dangers.

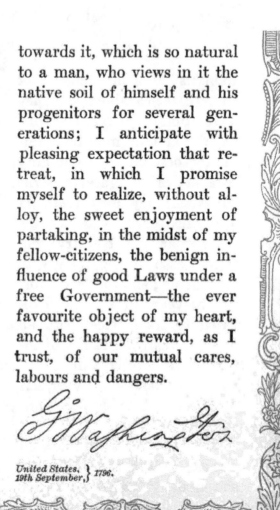

United States, } 1796.
19th September,}

Printed in the USA
CPSIA information can be obtained
at www.ICGtesting.com
LVHW011341061023
760261LV00005B/255